MW00881933

The Guide

By Robin A. Price

Printed in the United States of America

Unless otherwise indicated, Bible quotations are
taken from the King James Version of the Holy Bible.

Front Cover

"Image, used under license from Shutterstock.com"

The

Guide

And the Lord shall guide thee continually,

and satisfy your *soul*...Isaiah 58:11a

Table of Contents

POEM	Who Am I	5
Chapter 1	The Guide	7
Chapter 2	Poem	11
Chapter 3	The Call	12
Chapter 4	Remember	14
Chapter 5	Turning Points	21
Chapter 6	The Memo	45
Chapter 7	Heavenly Memo	59
Chapter 8	Job Description	64
Chapter 9	Opportunity	70
Chapter 10	I Apologize	82
Chapter 11	Why the Guide	89
Chapter 12	Bible Study	98
Chapter 13	Discovery	108
Chapter 14	Forgive Me!	112
Chapter 15	Peer Pressure	126
Chapter 16	Who's in Control?	130
Chapter 17	Walk Softly	136
Conclusion	Final Thoughts	146

Your "Life" matters to God, therefore;

at any cost, He will pursue YOU!

Love never quits!

~The Price has been PAID~

Preface

It wasn't until I spent 15 years of my life serving in Prison Ministry that 'the Guide' became relevant. I was set back! I was captured by a thought of losing a generation of young people to alcohol, drugs, perversion, the streets, cunning people, prison and so forth; if someone didn't warn them about life's mysteries and truths. That with choices; comes consequences! With poor vision, well; poor decisions are made. The question came to mind, who's looking into the future of our children, their tomorrow? Who's concerned about our young people who cry out daily for attention, and to start the journey of life?

The Guide Book was written to empower, strengthen, and to spring a ray of hope in the hearts and minds of young people as well as to parents. It is important that we "Never try to solve a problem independent of the very source it needs" *Robin Price-Boyd.* All hands should be on deck! The notion that it takes a village to raise children has truth! The notion that God is real, and we cannot live a successful life without Him is true!

As you read though 'the Guide book,' you will find insights and compelling information that should alter your path of life. If not, there will be real consequences doing it your way. Living life from the hip or by the seat of your pants will ultimately cost you! The good book of Wisdom says it this way, with no guide every person did what was right in their own eyes! Another passage says this, there is a way that seems right unto a person, but the end thereof will lead to destruction. Independence should not trump intra-dependence. We are wired to have a relationship with God. After all,

God did create us! Living apart from Him opens the door to a chaotic life, misery, turmoil and emptiness. Can the *creature* say to the Creator; I have no need of you? As a young person, you will need a GUIDE so buckle up, choose wisely, learn well; discover the mysteries of life, and why you are special in HIS eyes.

WHO AM I

I have given you a part of me saith the Lord.

I have shown you who I AM,

I have given to you insight and

the ability to understand.

How LORD?

By the hearing ear

By my guided hand

By the seeing eye

And

By your legs in which stand!

Who am I?

Although, I have not a physical body, I AM.

My majesty is in the earth in you,

saith the LORD.

I have given to you a part of me

that you may know who I AM.

Author
Robin A. Price-Boyd

Did you know?

Romans 1:20

"For the invisible things of him from the creation of the world are clearly seen, being understood by the things that are made, even his eternal power and Godhead; so that they _(You)_ are without excuse..."

Wow!

You are wired to know God!

THE GUIDE

The Guide was devised to aid and assist young people from the ages of 13 to 25 of how to live a successful life away from home. That means away from parental guidance and counsel; that means away from an instructional environment and supervision; that means away from rules and regulations that normally would be set by parents, a family member or the adult care taker.

Young teens and young adults often cry out for experience. That often times mean, they no longer desire parental supervision. That often times mean, "I'm grown now and I can handle it. That often means, "I know what I am doing; trust me, I will not make the same mistakes as you did (mom/dad)."

It's not that they do not need parental guidance but rather space to explore; time to figure life out, even to scratch the itch that runs deep into their soul. Dad and Mom should not take this kind of attitude or position personal. This posture is a mere sign that "*your child*" is crying out for the experience that only life can teach them. Ready or not, it's show time!

Remember what the book of wisdom said, "Train up a child in the way he (she) should go: and when he (she) is old, he (she) will not depart from it." Well, that my brothers and sisters reflects a season of time, a window of opportunity, and intentional preparation for what's to come. I hope you took advantage of that "window" span.

Because the "*Guide Book*" is biblically based, your child, teen, or young adult can now glean and learn to hear instruction from the Lord. Why is that important? I thought you would never ask.

Children glean and learn all the time! What they see with their eyes, what they hear with their ears, what they do with their hands, and where they walk with their feet, can be impactful...finding their way is a part of God's Plan. The "great" discovery of who they are in God and the "great" discovery of who they are without Him is yet a mystery. Experience sometimes is the best teacher; and since they are crying out to travel on life's journey, let them take the "GUIDE."

Perhaps now is a good time to share briefly with you about "Choices" and "Consequences;" about "Accountability" and "Ownership." Each of these choice words will become viable and meaningful along your child's journey...on this road called "Life." God will make plain these terms and create situations that will arouse the senses of your child (young people)...this generation! He will guide them with His eye and direct their path. Don't worry; it's all a part of His plan. As you read the "Guide book" this will make better sense to you. Remember, it is written: "How precious are His thoughts towards us? How great is the sum of them (Psalm 139:17)! If we could ever get a hold of what the Lord is really saying....His "Love" is O' so real!

POEM

~The Journey to Discovery~

Dear sons and daughters, because I love you
I will set you free

Because my Son died for you
I will wait patiently

Discover, discover along the way
How I've <u>guided</u> you every step of the way

On your journey
You may call upon ME at any time
Because I know that you are truly <u>mine</u>

Now your experience will be tailor made
So, whenever you need understanding
call to ME...your Creator and your Aide

So begin your journey as you please
for my guiding light will bring you ease

Please know that this process of discovery is
necessary...It's important to ME that you
understand I am not a "fairy,"

Just a loving God who sent a Savior
(Jesus Christ) to bring you home to ME!

Author, Robin A. Price-Boyd

THE CALL~

My sons and daughters, the Guide was written to help you find your way along life's journey. As you explore different things, seek new ventures, experience the ups and downs, and the highs and lows of life, remember; that I am just a **call** away, saith the Lord.

The Clarion Call!

- *Psalm 50:15~*

Call *upon me in the day of trouble...*

- *Jeremiah 33:3~*

***"Call** unto me, and I will answer thee, and show you great and mighty things, which you know not."*

- *Romans 10:13*

"For *whosoever shall **call** upon the name of the Lord shall be saved."*

You may call anytime, anywhere and any place!

*Liken unto the men and women in the Bible days...since the beginning of time; men and women began **calling** on the name of the LORD (Genesis 4:26). <u>Why not you?</u>*

- *Isaiah 55:6*

***Call** my brother, my sister upon the Lord while He is near...*

Let us begin~

REMEMBER~

A man or woman can only give you as best they can the wisdom from what life has dealt to them, their personal struggles, personal defeats and yes, even their personal victories. So, don't hold them accountable if they have not told you the whole truth. Don't hold them accountable if they do not play the 'spade' or 'ace in the hole' card to bail you out of your personal situations. The maze, triangle or cob web you find yourself in is designed to help you discover your true delivering source…God. Man's (woman's) goings are of the Lord; how can a man/woman then understand his/her own way? Proverbs 20:24

Remember the Source!

God said learn to look to Him for everything that you may need. Learn early in your walk or journey and in the discovery process, and you are well on your way to finding Him when those challenging life situations present themselves.

I was thirty six when I came to know the Lord. I recall vividly how he beckoned me to come; how he wooed me into His arms; and boy, was I so ready! He used seasons of breakdowns; seasons of mourning, seasons of loss, and seasons of cast away. I travailed like a pregnant woman ready for delivery.

Well with you, it might be something different. God knows each of us personally! He knows the right formula to get us to our desired end. Psalm 139:13 states, God "possessed your reins; He covered you in your mother's womb." You were fashioned by the Master's hands and made in secret! And let's not forget, you were created in His image, Hmmm! Jeremiah 29:11 states, "For

I know the thoughts that I think toward you, saith the Lord, thoughts of peace, and not of evil, to give you an expected end." (One Bible translation states, a hope and a future.) Wow! It is no wonder the Lord takes an interest in guiding us.

It wasn't until I saw how personal God was that I came to understand His love, His mercy, and His compassion for each of us. Perhaps if you knew that the Lord knows what you are thinking (Psalm 139:4); He knows your down sitting and uprising (Psalm 139:2); He is acquainted with all your ways (Psalm 139:3); He even knows the number of hairs on your head (Matthew 10:30). Listen, God said you are fearfully and wonderful made (Psalm 139:14). I can't wait until you discover all of who He is and how much He loves "you" personally.

Are you ready? **Let's begin!**

Every parent should prepare their child to know the Lord in the most common and most fundamental way:

Through our Senses

(Taste*Touch*Smell*Hearing*Seeing)

Through Feelings and Emotions

(Love*Joy*Peace*Gentleness)

Through our Body...both outer & inner

(Physical~Mental~Emotional~Relational)

Through our Human side

(Breathe*Heart*Flesh and Blood)

In spirit and not only flesh

God is Spirit!

<u>Examples In Scripture:</u>

Why would God identify himself to us in the following ways?

He Sees	Jeremiah 23:34
He Looks	Psalm 14:2
He Hears	Psalm 17:6
He Smells	Genesis 8:21
He has a Voice	Psalm 29
He Speaks	Isaiah 45:19
He Remembers	Genesis 8:1
We can Taste Him	Psalm 34:8 Hmm!
He has a Heart	Genesis 6:6
He has an Arm	Psalm 89:20-21
He has a Hand	Isaiah 49:16

There are plenty of scriptures that define God and His identity to us. Why would He make this plain in His Word (The Holy Bible)? Why would he plant such profound scriptures that speak to our very existence? Perhaps the following scriptures could shed light:

"And God said, let us make man in our **image**, after our likeness…" **(Genesis 1:26)**

"In the day that God created man, in the **likeness** of God made he him; male and female created he them: and blessed them…" **(Genesis 5:1-2)**

"…I shall be satisfied, when I awake, with thy **likeness**…" **(Psalm 17:15)**

"Therewith bless we God, even the Father, and therewith curse we men, which are made after the **similitude** of God."
(James 3:9)

To any event, God was trying to say something to us through the scriptures. He wanted us to know that He was and is real. He wants us to understand that He is alive! Our very existence rests upon who He is. What that means is this, YOU are somebody! YOU have purpose! YOU are fearfully and wonderfully made by the mere fact that _YOU are in His likeness_.

Scripture says from the womb of your mother God possessed your inward parts and covered you (Psalm 139:13). Isn't that amazing? The Creator of the universe, the one who made heaven and earth, defined us from day one… hmm!

Having said that, let's break down our development stages in growth. Let's see the "turning points" that were crucial in our growth. Why is this important? Sometimes we have to go back so that we can go forward. ☺

~Turning Points~

(SEVEN Levels plus ONE)

1. New Born to 18 months
2. 18 months to 3 years of age
3. 4 to 6 years of age
4. 7 to 10 years of age
5. 11 to 14 years of age
6. 15 to 17 years of age
7. 18 to 21 years of age
8. 21 and older (Adult Age)

It's Show Time!

It is no wonder the Lord shared in His Word the following Scriptures about the Father, Mother, and Child. Each family member has a part to play in the rearing of a child. What's your part? Let's see!

THE MOTHER

(1)   1 Timothy 5:14

"I will therefore that the younger women marry, bear children, ***guide the house*** (manage their home), be the head of (rule) the family or the house...give no one reason to find fault or to speak shamefully."

(2)   Titus 2:3 – 5

"The aged women likewise, that they be in behavior as becometh holiness, not false accusers, not given to much wine, teachers of good things;"

That they may teach the young women to be:

A.   Sober
B.   To love their husbands
C.   To *love their children*
D.   To be discreet

E.   Chaste (pure)

F.   *Keepers at home*

G.   Good

H.   Obedient to their own
husbands~

Why?

That the <u>word of God</u> be not insulted or not reverenced…or accused…blamed.

<u>The Greek Translation </u>of "Keepers at home #3626 - Oikouros- from oikos 3624…means o*ne who looks after domestic affairs with prudence and care, meaning (cautious and good care). Care to know Hebrew – Greek?*

(3)   **Proverbs 22:6**

A mother should train up her child in the way he (she) should go: filling the mind, instructing or educating. Initiate the child's learning and start them on the right path. Teaching the truth according to scripture:

Here are two Examples~

Ecclesiastes 11:9

Rejoice, O young one, in thy youth; and **1** – Let your heart cheer thee in the days of thy youth, and **2** – Walk in the ways of your heart, and **3** – in the sight of your eyes: but know this; that for all these things God will bring you into judgment. Hmm!

Ecclesiastes 11:10

States, therefore…A – <u>remove sorrow</u> from your heart and B <u>– put away evil</u> from your flesh and C – learn that childhood and youth are vanity (empty) without purpose.

A mother should protect their child from sorrow; and to keep evil from the flesh, and to empower their children (warn) of foolish living. A childish state of mind (unlearned) can be dangerous and cause much pain.

5 Components for Mom to Monitor:

A.   *Spiritual Growth*

Prayer time, praise &reading God's Word
(Church)

B.   *Physical Growth*

How to care for the body &nourishment

C.   *Emotional Growth*

The care of feelings/emotions...mannerisms

D.   *Relational Growth*

How children relate to others in/out of home

E.   *Mental Growth*

Where are they intellectually...thought life!

The second part of **Proverbs 22:6** states and
when he (she) gets old, they will not depart
from the training learned. While they may
experiment with life's whining road, they
will come to their senses and revert back to

the training. I personally can attest to this truth. God has a way of reminding us of what we were taught growing up from our parents, grandparents, elders and those who might have had responsibility over our personal growth and development.

Holistic training is crucial...be open to helping your child grow properly in all areas. If he or she lacks proper development, it will show up down the road, around the corner, beyond the trees and into the forest (years later).

The second part of **Proverbs 22:6** states a promise...*and when he or she is old, they will not depart from it (the training).* Mom has a crucial role in rearing up her child (children); unfortunately, many mothers miss this somehow. Children go under developed and malnourished, lacking vital impartation and guidance. Can you assess your own personal experience in your home? What was missing for you?

List here please:

(1) Spiritual developments

(2) Peace in the home

(3) Being an example before you

(4) Intellectual developments

(5) Respects

Some helpful hints to think about are...

Love
Discipline
Respect
Peace in the home
Responsibility
Holistic training
 A sense of Belonging
Spiritual development
Intellectual development
Relational development
Emotional development
Proper regard for feelings
Having a "choice"
Being an example before you

THE FATHER

1 Timothy 3:4

Dad… Rule well your house, having your children in *subjection* with all honesty. (KJV)

Dad…Manage your house well, keeping your children *under control* with all dignity. (NAS)

Dad… Manage your family well and see that your *children obey you* with proper respect. (NIV)

- Subjection
- Under Control
- Obedience and Respect

Ephesians 6:4

"**Fathers**, provoke not your children to wrath: but bring them up in the *nurture* and *admonition* of the Lord." (KJV)

"**Fathers**, do not provoke your children to anger; but bring them up in the *discipline* and *instruction* of the Lord." (NAS)

"**Fathers**, do not exasperate your children; instead, bring them up in the *training* and instruction of the Lord." (NIV)

Did you take note of the BIG Five?

- Nurture
- Admonition
- Discipline
- Instruction
- Training

I hope you did! Exasperate means – to irritate greatly… to annoy keenly… vexation of spirit.

The Lord clearly gives specific instruction to the father for rearing children.

As you can see, the father's role is just as important as the mother's. Care to share what your experience was like in your home? Care to talk with God about what you liked and disliked? He is listening!

List here please:

(1) Leader

(2) Poor example

(3) Regard for your feelings

(4) Role Model

(5) Responsible

Some helpful hints to think about...

Absent/missing
Good example/Poor example
Role Model
Disciplined
Regard for your feelings
Responsible
Good provider for the family
Leader

Dad generally imparts the tough, discipline and authoritative components needed for your growth & development.

If your father was not in the home, how vital was it to your upbringing? If your father was in the house, how well did he keep with the instructions God provided above? Perhaps you had another male adult play the role of your dad, how impactful was that to you…did they miss the mark? Whatever the situation may have been in your life, I hope the above scriptures brought insight of how vital the role of Dad and Mom plays in the home.

Words of Encouragement!

"When my father and mother forsake me, then the Lord will take me up" *(Psalm 27:10).*

"For God's eyes are upon the ways of every man (woman), and He sees all things" *(Job 34:21).*

"For I know the thoughts that I think toward you, saith the Lord, thoughts of peace…" *(Jeremiah 29:11),* ponder this as you reflect.

THE CHILD

The roles of both the father and mother are vital (important). Your upbringing has an effect on your personal outcome. If either parent neglected to nourish you (the child) properly, there were and are consequences. The Bible offers insightful knowledge of how each parent should have reared, developed, groomed, and nourished you (their child), *see pages 25 – 32.*

Because the Bible gives explicit (vivid) and clear definition to what kind of discipline is needed to keep children safe, it was and still is important for every parent to read the Bible. Unfortunately, if mom or dad neglected to receive God's insight, they probably missed the mark (fell short) of rearing, developing, grooming and properly nourishing you (the child)!

So how do we make up for missed time? You might even ask, can we make up for lost time? Great question! God redeems the time (see Colossians 4:5 & Ephesians 5:16). God designed within you a "set time" for knowing the truth...harden not your heart when you hear His voice speaking...*your conscience will be your guide.*

Did you find it interesting that at age 2 you could get away with more than when you reached the age 6? Did you realize that by the time you were 10, you became more accountable as well as responsible for helping out around the house? By mere virtue, trial and error, and what your eye gate saw in the home, what your ear gate was allowed to hear behind closed doors; there was a constant demand upon your growth...knowing right from wrong. In addition, what about the rules established in the home? One way or another, you were responsible for growing up, right?

Right now, I am thinking about choices and consequences. Did you know that choices and consequences were designed to enhance or stretch your intellectual development? I tell you the truth, God is working all the time. He knows all about the challenges you will face and have faced. As you continue to grow, remember this; the "CHOICE" you make God will not interfere with. True Love does not meddle with the Choice. True Love allows you to find your way. True Love waits patiently for you to make better CHOICES. True Love allows you the opportunity to be chastened (corrected) through CONSEQUENCES. Your **senses** will be heightened and alarmed when a **consequence** manifest (made known) from the choice that you made…at least it is supposed to be.☺

Consider this for a moment, the beating you were warned about at an early age…did it alarm your senses of the pain to come?

When you did something worth being praised, did you like the pleasant reward or thank you? How about when someone said; I appreciate that, you were very considerate. Or, how about that $5.00 bill you received for doing something good…how did that make you feel? Those moments were designed to help you figure out or discern right from wrong or good from evil. The *power of choice* is forever before YOU.

Now would be a good time to give you some scriptures from the Bible. Turn with me to **Proverbs 22:15**, "foolishness is bound in the heart of a child; but the rod of correction shall drive it far from him/her." The rod of correction (beaten) is designed to deal with "foolishness." How else are you/children supposed to know right from wrong…that doing wrong has consequences? If God said a child or children has foolishness in their heart, well, wouldn't He know?

For a moment, examine your childhood and share with me? What do you remember? List at least 3 to 5 incidents that you can recall your parents/authority figure dealt with you about. What foolish things did you do? Be Honest.

(1) Kissing A boy in Kinder-garden in the cubby .

(2) Talking too much in School

.

(3) Cursing @ parents

.

(4) _____

_____

_____.

(5) _____

_____

_____.

So, what do you think? Were you honest about the incident or situation? Were you warned 1st and/or did you ignore the warnings given to you before continuing to do something foolish?

Take a look at **Proverbs 23:13-14**, I will paraphrase this one. Look, do not withhold correcting your child, if you beat him/her, they will not die; matter of fact, you will save them from destruction. Question? Would you say it is better to beat the child early or for them to continue on a destructive path? Every parent has to make that choice.

Good parenting is real and needs to be in place in every home. The lack of good parenting can be very costly for any child. Can you determine which parenting style your parent/authority figure used in your home? Be truthful!

(A) Permissive Parenting   _____

(B) Intentional Parenting   _____

(C) Neglectful Parenting   *Mom*

(D) Authoritarian Parenting   *DAD*

Care to know the difference? Let's see!

I.   One breathes rebellion

II.   One breathes cooperation

III.   One breathes destruction

IV.   One breathes passiveness

Each parenting style has consequences and creates either a negative or positive outcome for the child/children. Unfortunately, sometimes parents rear their children as they were reared or raised…Hmm!

Take an assessment of your childhood. Where are you today? What has your life breathed or demonstrated (manifested)? Your behavior will tell it all! **List the parenting style here:**

Proverbs 20:11 states "Even a child is known by his doings, whether his work be pure, and whether it be right." In other words, a child's ways and actions will be revealed…their motives uncovered.

Your outcome, behavior, actions, motives and so forth are a direct affect from your childhood experiences, exposure, parental style and the list goes on and on. It is no wonder Scripture states to train up a child in the way he/she should go (God's way). It is no wonder parents are admonished to guide their children early…at onset…in the very beginning from the womb!

Parents can only teach what they have learned and understood. This is not about the blame game but rather about making better choices <u>now</u> for a brighter future. God is available 24-7. Now matters!

Open the Book! Start afresh! Become wise through God's Word! He redeems the time! It is never too late in Him!

Parenting Styles (Answers)

Permissive parenting- breathes rebellion
Intentional parenting- breathes cooperation
Neglectful parenting- breathes destruction
Authoritarian parenting-breathes passiveness

You can learn more about parenting styles online. Sometimes a deeper look into the subject matter can offer further clarification and insights. Take full advantage of probing and digging further to obtain the right perspective on parenting. And whatever you do, please consider God's Word in the mix of your study. I trust what we have discussed here is sufficient to stir your curiosity. **Deuteronomy 29:29,** tells us that God reveals the secret things…those secret things learned are to be passed down to the next generation (your children).

In life you will learn that there are three (3) ways of doing things:

- Your Way
- The World's Way
- God's Way

The CHOICE is yours to make!

THE GUIDE:

Psalm 32:8

"I will instruct thee and teach thee in the way which thou shalt go: I will **guide** thee with my eye, saith the Lord." With God having such a stake in humankind …seeing we were created in His image, in His likeness and similitude; do you perceive it is only right that He takes interest in our lives to guide us, advise us, counsel us, admonish us, and direct our path?

What are your thoughts about the Mother and Father's role? (Remember, there are no wrong answers to this question, just an opportunity for you to express your level of understanding and to be frank/open with the Lord).

Jot down your thoughts on the next page…be honest.

Mom was present + didn't teach me anything about being a woman, (bathing, cleaning, sex) nothing. Not a good role model. Dad was busy working like a dog everyday - family man yet lacked emotion.

_____

_____

_____

_____

_____

_____

_____

_____

_____

_____

_____.

The Scripture says, "Come, let us reason with God." Let's talk about how we (you) feel and share truthfully one with another. The Lord wants *you* to understand Him, His position, His truth, and His ways of doing things (Isaiah 1:18a). There you will find safety, peace and have a refuge.

DID YOU GET THE MEMO?

How interesting is it when we discover that we are not always in the loop of things? That the "memo" our friends received, we did not get. No one took the time to share the pertinent information with us... or tell us "like it T I is."

Well, here is one for the road. A secret that every child, boy and girl should be informed about, or at least guided to this truth! Here is the big question, How Does God see YOU, as a child (children)? To help answer this question, scripture guides us in different angles so that we can see the whole picture from God's point of view. Let's take a look...

God <u>sees</u> Children through the Scriptures:

(1) Out of the mouth of babes and suckling's hast thou ordained strength~

(2) Lo, children are a heritage of the Lord: and the fruit of the womb is his reward~

(3) As arrows are in the hand of a mighty man; so are children of the youth~

(4) Children's children are the crown of old men; and the glory of children are their fathers~

(5) Happy is the man that hath his quiver full of them (you are a blessing)

(6) Suffer little children, and forbid them not, to come unto me: for of such is the kingdom of heaven.

-Read Psalms and Proverbs-

God <u>informs</u> Parents through the Scriptures:

(1)   …for childhood and youth are vanity

(2)   …a wise son makes a glad father: but a foolish son is the heaviness of his mother

(3)   …but a child left to himself brings his mother shame

(4)   A wise son makes a glad father; but a foolish son despises his mother

(5)   A foolish son is a grief to his father, and bitterness to her that bare him

(6)   A foolish son is the calamity of his father…

-Read Proverbs-

God <u>informs</u> Children through the Scriptures:

(1)   ...for childhood and youth are vanity

(2)   Children obey your parents in all things: for this is well pleasing unto the Lord.

(3)   Honor thy father and thy mother: that thy days may be long upon the land which the Lord thy God giveth thee.

(4)   Foolishness is bound in the heart of a child; but the rod of correction shall drive it far from him/her.

(5)   There is a way that appears right unto a person, but the end thereof are; the ways of destruction.

-Read Ecclesiastes and Proverbs-

God <u>admonishes</u> Parents through the Scriptures:

(1)   He that spares his rod hateth his son: but he that loves him chastens him betimes (meaning quickly).

(2)   Chasten thy son while there is hope, and let not thy soul spare for his crying.

(3)   Even a child is known by his doings, whether his/her work be pure, and whether it be right.

(4)   Train up a child in the way he/she should go: and when he/she is old, he/she will not depart from it.

(5)   Withhold not correction from the child: for if thou beatest him with the rod, he/she shall not die...his/her soul shall be delivered from hell.

-Read Proverbs-

(6)   And, ye Father's, provoke not your children to wrath: but bring them up in the nurture and admonition of the Lord *(Ephesians 6:4; Psalm 78:4-7).*

Now that you have the *MEMO*, study it, memorize it; share it if you like.   More importantly, begin to let the **memo** guide you. You are now in the loop! You now have a peek-a-boo of what God intended from the very beginning for your life as a child.

I thought it was interesting how God broke down in scripture and outlined each segment of responsibility to the corresponding person…the father, the mother and the child. Everyone can take their appropriate places and respond accordingly to what God was attempting to convey through His Word. Use this ***GUIDE!***

The Memo matters!   What are your thoughts now regarding God's Word to you? Please share your thoughts on the next page:

Have you ever heard of the saying, **"Knowledge is powerful?"** *Yes or No* Isn't that why people go to college and further their education to gain knowledge and insight about a specific topic of interest or to become wiser in their profession? Knowledge equals power? *Yes or No*

How might your life have changed if you
knew about the "Memo" early in life?

_____

_____

_____

_____

_____

_____

_____

_____

_____

What might you have done differently had
you known about the scriptures that speak to
your responsibility as a child?

_____

_____

_____

_____

_____

If you have ever been invited to Church...the above is why, so that you might gain knowledge of God, His way, and the TRUTH of how things really are "suppose" too be. After all, you are going to be judged based on TRUTH. That is why the discovery of God is so vital. I personally do not blame you for why you are where you are today. Anyone void of the TRUTH will find themselves in some pretty strange and awkward places in life.

When I was growing up, it was this saying... "She/he is looking for love in all the wrong places." Have you ever heard of this saying? Finding love is likened unto finding a needle in a hay stack. Love comes in many different forms (1) Agape, (2) Eros and (3) Philo, etc. In your spare time, look up those words. How might you know which of the above terms you have experienced?

Agape love is something most people never truly experience because they end up settling for less than... and don't bother to ask them (people) to compare Agape...as you cannot compare something if you have never experienced it?

Did You Know

The TRUTH brings to light what is hidden from the naked eye. The TRUTH exposes dark things. The TRUTH sets us free. The TRUTH makes way for bigger and brighter things. When God sent Jesus to the earth, He sent Jesus to bear witness to the TRUTH. God sent Jesus that we might experience an abundant life, a fulfilled heart, and more importantly, an opportunity to have an experience with Agape Love (God Himself).

The Church is the ground and pillar for the TRUTH of GOD. The MEMO is the TRUTH and is expressed from the posture of LOVE. It has nothing to do with control. Out of our experience through the Word of God, we find what being fulfilled is all about…we dance and sing because the Word is our inspiration and guide. We commit and serve because we are grateful for the opportunity to live in the land of the living. **I would caution you to stop just existing and learn to LIVE.**

The Bible is full of MEMOs. These Memos are waiting to be read by you. Memo's for direction, a Memo of joy and peace; Memo's to keep you away from danger; Memo's which will bring you into prosperity; Memo's for guidance into relationships and marriage; Memo's for health. Memo's on how to raise children and Memo's on how to have a successful life, etc.

Now that I am writing this book, I think it would be good to start a Memo Ministry…☺ No seriously, check this out~

MEMO Title: Boundaries and Hedged In… So, do you really believe that you are in control? I will definitely give you the answer to that question. But not yet just think about it for a moment!

You can follow the clues in the Word of God…

A.   Job 3:23 states, "Why is light given to a man or woman whose way is hedged in?"

B.   Job 19:8 states, "He hath fenced up my way that I cannot pass, and he hast set darkness in my paths." Hmm!

C.   Proverbs 16:9 states, a man's (woman's) heart deviseth (plans) his/her way: but the Lord directeth their steps.

D.   Proverbs 20:24 states, a man's (woman's) goings are of the Lord; how can either of them understand their own way?

E.   Jeremiah 23:10 states, O Lord, I know that the way of a man (woman) is not in him (her): it is not in him (her) that walketh to direct their own steps.

So, I ask you again, do you really believe you are in control? Keep living and you will discover this truth for yourself. Don't take my word for it as LOVE will make Himself known to you!

Let's look at another Memo namely, *the Heavenly Employment Memo*! What does it take to work in the Kingdom of God? What are some of the prerequisites? How do you get started? And much, much more!

HEAVENLY EMPLOYMENT MEMO

(PREREQUISITE)

God sent Jesus, His only begotten Son to earth to save us (you). **Acts 3:26** states, Unto you first God, having raised up his Son Jesus, sent him to bless you (me), in turning away every one of us (you) from our iniquities (sins). **Acts 4:12** therefore solidifies this stating, "Neither is there salvation in any other; for there is none other name under heaven given among men, whereby we must be saved."

Salvation is a gift from God. One *prerequisite* of the Father therefore to be employed by Him is to accept this gift called Salvation. **Romans 6:23** tells us "For the wages of sin is death; but the gift of God is eternal life through Jesus Christ our Lord."

Once that is established, we are eligible to be employed by God. Now it is important to remember, Salvation is the initial step. **Second**, we want to be empowered to live and to handle the work that God has ordained for us to do. Even as Jesus was anointed with the Holy Spirit (**Acts 10:38**), we must now be baptized with the Holy Spirit, as well.

Our example of Jesus' Baptism is expressed in **Matthew 3:13**. The Scripture reads as follows: "Then cometh Jesus from Galilee to Jordan unto John, to be baptized of him." While *John the Baptist* initially resisted what Jesus was asking of him, Jesus replied saying, "Suffer it to be so for now: for thus it becometh us to fulfill all righteousness."

Jesus understood his job description from Heaven. His employment obligation to

God was to "fulfill all righteousness" because he knew he was setting an example of what we would need to do as followers. This example "the Baptism of the Holy Spirit" was crucial to get any JOB done on earth for God.

Now, note this; God gives His Spirit to those who will obey Him. **Acts 5:32** sheds light on this truth, "...and so is also the Holy Ghost, whom God hath given to them that obey him." It is imperative that we take note of this passage of Scripture. The power won't come, the power cannot be, the power will never manifest without a heart change to "OBEY" the Father (God).

Scripture tells us in **2 Chronicles 16:9** "For the eyes of the Lord run to and fro throughout the whole earth, to show himself strong in the behalf of them whose heart is perfect toward him." 'Perfect' in this context of Scripture refers to complete, wholeness.

In **1Samuel 16:7**, we find that God does not see man as we do, "for man looketh on the outward appearance, but the Lord looketh on the heart (the inward part of you and I)," *(the "th" simply means continually).*

Early on in the Gospels of Matthew, Mark and Luke, Jesus exclaims he must preach the kingdom of God to neighboring cities and towns because that was where he was sent by God. His *Job* was to reach as many people as would hear him (*Matthew 4:17-25; Mark 1:38; Luke 4:43*). In **John 5:17,** Jesus said the Father works and I work also.

In **Luke 4:18**, Jesus mentions that the Spirit of the Lord is upon him, because he was anointed to preach the gospel to the poor; he was sent to heal the broken hearted, he was to preach deliverance to those who were captive, and to open blinded eyes, to set at liberty those who were hurt, and to preach the coming of the year of our Lord.

How awesome! Jesus just gave an overview of his "Employment Description;" his assignment in the earth. Likewise, we have an assignment from God, and that assignment can come into existence upon the empowering gift of the Holy Spirit. Now, no doubt the Holy Spirit is in the earth for several reasons and has several functions, but for sure, he helps us to do our JOBS in the earth.

JOB DESCRIPTION

In case you didn't know this, you are needed in the Kingdom of God. If you ever find yourself wanting to belong or need something to do, or want a JOB, then you are welcome here! There is something for everyone in the Kingdom of God.

Never sell yourself short, never feel inferior, never think that you don't have what it takes; never think that you are alone! When I first discovered this in the Bible, it blessed me. I want to now share it with you. You will undoubtedly find people in this world who will try to belittle you, try to make you feel less than, try to put you down for their own self ego. God said you are just as significant as the next person. In Him, we are all needed to be complete and to function as a whole in His Kingdom.

In 1 Corinthians 12 God uses the physical body as an analogy of how He put parts of the body together and how they were intended to help, to support for the complete functioning of the entire body. He uses the eye and the ear, the hand and the foot; each carrying significance to the whole body.

Imagine your hand telling your foot it's not needed. Imagine your eye telling you ear, go away. Crazy right! So liken unto us as a part of God's body in His Kingdom. You have significance! You matter! Your part in the Kingdom is vital! Your work and the territory God has set aside for you from the foundation of the world await you. Matter of fact, God tells us in this same Chapter, the weaker of us is more important than the stronger of us. It's true!

thians 12:24 states God
...ody together, having given
more abundant honor to the part which
lacked. In verse 25, He explains why, "that
there should be no schism in the body, but
that the members in His Kingdom should
have the same care one for another"...hum.
You are just as important as the next person
in God's Kingdom. We all have something
to do! If you want a job, it's yours. Look
again at the prerequisite and go for it.

The following job description gives
an overview of the areas of importance to
effectively handle your (my) Heavenly
position (job) on the earth.

- Go ye therefore, and teach all nations
  (people)*(Matthew 28:19)*
- Pray without ceasing *(1Thessa. 5:17)*
- Live by Faith *(Romans 1:17b)*
- Study to be quiet... *(1Thessa. 4:11)*

- Study to shew thyself approved unto God...*(2 Timothy 2:15)*
- ...be thou an example of the believers...*(1Timothy 4:12)*
- ...give attendance to reading... *(1Timothy 4:13)*
- Hold fast to the form of sound words... *(2 Timothy 1:13)*
- Fight the good fight of faith, lay hold on eternal life...*(1 Timothy 6:12)*
- Walk in wisdom toward them that are without *(Colossians 4:5)*
- Let your speech be always with grace...*(Colossians 4:6)*
- And whatsoever ye do, do it heartily, as to the Lord...*(Colossians 3:23)*

There are other duties as assigned however; the above scriptures are key functions for every believer to help manage their job position in the Kingdom of God.

The Bible declares in **Matthew 9:37-38** that "The harvest truly is plenteous, but the *laborers* (workers) are few." In the next verse you see Jesus saying "Pray therefore the Lord of the harvest, that he will send forth *laborers* into his harvest."

As we obey, God will continue to add gifts, the anointing, helpers, and finances to get the job done. Your position and gift to the Body of Christ is crucial and relevant, so please consider what's at stake. People are waiting on YOU. *God pays well!*

I compel you to add scriptures to this job description as you are prompted by the Holy Spirit to do so. Because "You" are tailor-made for a specific audience and people; more may be required of you to get the job done.

For example, Ye are witnesses of God (**Isaiah 43:12**), what does that entail, and Fear thou not (**Isaiah 41:10**) as you go forward to get His work done in the Kingdom. Imagine that, I thought I was done and just as I was ending my thought, God said to add these two Job descriptions. He always bears witness to what He is trying to convey for clarity and precision. Hallelujah!

**Remember, your Job will align with your God given purpose in life!

OPPORTUNITY

I have had the **opportunity** to work with sixteen (16) young men. It was interesting how we met. I would have never imaged what God was doing had He not unctioned me to write this book. So this experience I walked through was for you!

Imagine, sixteen souls, sixteen personalities, sixteen mannerisms, sixteen attitudes and of course, sixteen different characters to learn on a basketball team; yes, I said basketball team. The energy was high, the games were intense, everyone wanted to play the game and everyone wanted to win. Most of these guys slept and ate basketball (that's a figure of speech); in other words, they simply loved the game.

Now imagine this, these guys had played street ball for years. These guys had known one another for quite some time. I was the new kid on the block....attempting to come into their space.

What were their ages? I thought you would never ask...try 18 to 26 years of age. These guys had their own mindset, their own way of seeing things, their own way of playing the game which they loved so much. Competition is on! If you know anything about young men, then you should know that their egos were high and they liked to show off. Well that comes with the game, doesn't it?

So here was my challenge! How do I get sixteen young men to convert from "street ball" to "organized ball" or even play as a team? Each of them had talent. They were well capable of being real good ball players. *In my mind, I'm thinking it shouldn't be that hard, right?* Well to my surprise, it took us more than eight games to figure this out. Matter of fact, it was bad. Instead of seeing an OPPORTUNITY, the guys had settled in their minds that the problem was not changing or converting to organized ball, but the problem was with one other. The blame game and pointing the finger at each other manifested.

Believe it or not, three guys resolved to quit the team. Two of them stopped showing up for the games, while the other one quit after having a poor game performance. Perhaps these guys had no vision, no commitment, and no respect for the team as a whole. Perhaps they failed to see the OPPORTUNITY presented to them. Care to know what I mean by the term "OPPORTUNITY?"

Each day we have an OPPORTUNITY to validate what we

believe in, who we truly are as a person, and certainly an OPPORTUNITY to prove how much we love someone or something. **Love is an action word.** When you love someone or something (in this case basketball for the guys); there should have been hard evidence to toward that end.

I cannot tell you how many times I tried to communicate "**team ball**" while in the game. Play smart...keep your heads on straight! Listening was a huge problem. Following instructions proved to be a bigger problem. Yelling at them didn't work either. The guys were simply divided and played as they knew to play (street ball). The reset button seemed to always default to that end. Change was difficult! *With that said, as young people, watch your habits and the disciplines you form along the way. Be careful not to lock into old habits. Be* *open to becoming a better YOU! Change is possible! Remember, life will teach you to mature and to accept change for growth!*

O.k., back to what I was sharing: signs of disrespect, signs of discord, signs of not communicating, signs of mishandling one another, signs of giving up, signs of quitting...well that told me a lot without them having to say anything. The young men from day one had expressed how much they truly loved basketball. And yet, God revealed just the opposite.

Love will be tested. Love will push you to higher heights. Love will test your limits and limitations...your stamina and your endurance. *Here is what I discovered,* the hype, the excitement of playing the game (egos) and the rush (adrenalin) the guys felt on the court was the underling love for the game called "Basketball." These young men lacked fundamentals; they failed to transition

from street ball to organized ball. Further, respect, hard-work, teamwork, maturity, constructive criticism, precision, integrity, skill-set, development, and relationship or partnership (one with another) should have been formed at some point to build a solid basketball team for winning.

The OPPORTUNITY to come together as a unit to build something positive and meaningful was lost in the shuffle of individual play and selfishness of the game. I encouraged the guys to figure it out, talk things over, practice together as a team; work things out among themselves and find the solution to the problem to build a solid team.

I figured if they lose enough, they would come around. In hindsight, I'm not sure...after every game lost they were frustrated; embarrassed; and found blame in one another- wow! So, I'm not sure that was the best thing to do either. Needless to say, the love for the game dimmed. The puzzle was still unresolved. We plowed through animosity, selfishness, jealousy, discord and discontent...need I say more.

My position was this; I merely presented to the guys an OPPORTUNITY to come off the street into the gym to showcase their skill. So, did they have what it took? YES! Did they know they had what it takes, NO! **Discovering the solution is not always in front of us**. We sometimes have to go through the experience, the let downs, the disappointments, the frustrations and emotional highs and lows to find out what is in us, and to come to terms with our inadequacies. It is not until this point that we can regroup, rethink and reposition ourselves for better outcomes and hopefully good success.

I found out you cannot tell young people everything. Young people have to endure trial and error, plow through the misunderstandings, overcome pride; be transformed from a "show me" or Missouri state of mindset, in addition to handling their independence. Why...because hearing can be difficult, seeing can be difficult too, and by far, comprehension of matters that are challenging to them takes time to work through to say the least.

The mindset and state of being for young people is important! I am reminded of this wise saying, deal with "young people" according to knowledge, according to their state of mind/understanding. You can't rush maturity. Wisdom allows young people to discover themselves; where they are, and where they are not. At 13 - 18 years of age, there is much to consider with this generation. Highs and lows! Ups and downs! Ins and outs! The thinking, feeling and acting-out process of young people can be weighty and encumber some. Applying patience and walking out situations with them can prove to be profitable. God has a plan!

That attitude, resistance, last word, disrespect, opposition, aggressive behavior and so forth has a timeline. There is something on the horizon that God makes plain at an appointed time. His love endures all of that! His love brings the young generation into a knowing (eyes opened) a place called there! It's important to not rush God's process. It's important to allow "time" to deal with the heart, heart matters and the mindset of young people. The truth of the matter is that "time" allows for discovery! **Discovery is powerful and can be transformational!** Note I used ages 13 – 18 as a baseline but even 19 – 24 year olds are challenged with maturation. I often think about how long it took me to grow up and to reach my place called "**there**." Life has a way of teaching us a more excellent way of living. In other words; "**time**" and the exposure to real situations can open our eyes!

All I'm saying is this, rethink your OPPORTUNITIES, regroup and reposition yourselves to perceive and understand why an open door is presented to YOU. After all, no adult in their right mind truly desires to run your life if the truth be told. That is the last thing most adults want to do (at least most of us). *Ponder this for a moment:* could it be possible your loved one does not want you to make the same mistakes they made in life? Could it be possible they want a better future for you? Is it wrong for them to desire to save you from some of the drama and heartache that life can bring? Or could it be your loved one has a conscious, and this is a last **opportunity** to help you abort the hard road you are about to embark upon?

When an adult figure – be it parent, guardian, teacher, family or friend – begins to pour into you, take this **opportunity** and ask questions to those who seek to help and not offend. Take this **opportunity** to hear wisdom and glean from the experience of someone who has gone before you. Take this **opportunity** to be empowered to make a more intelligent decision; that's all. Ask what are their motives for sharing with you? Ask what are the benefits they gain from pouring out their heart? Ask why do they care? You will be surprised at the answers you might receive.

As a young person, you are going to get a lot of OPPORTUNTIES along the way. Look for them and make the most out of them. Embrace your OPPORTUNITIES and make them count. After all, you will have children one day and this will make a whole lot of sense to you then. ☺

By the way, our basketball record in the end was 3 − 9. We really should have been 7 − 5. We literally beat ourselves out of 4 games. Turnovers, missed free throws, lack of team playing and poor rebounding cost us dearly.

My personal take away from this basketball experience was that action speaks louder than words! To love something is to be willing "**to change**" to get the desired result one hopes to gain. When an **opportunity** presents itself to YOU, take full advantage of it (whatever the cost maybe).

I APOLOGIZE

While mediating and thinking about what would be the best way to impact your life; God spoke to my heart with this topic: "I apologize."

Often times I have *apologized* to my young audience every time I received the chance. So you may ask, WHY? The answer is quite simple and uncomplicated. When you think on the word "*apologizing*," what comes to mind? Something you did wrong, an offense, or mistreatment of someone; right? Perhaps a harsh word, a misunderstanding that went sour, or a poor reaction to something in the heat of the moment...whatever the case, we often find ourselves *apologizing* for something that was never intended on purpose.

As an adult, be it dad, mom, uncle, aunt, sister, brother, cousin, friend, teacher, etc.; I believe it is important to express our feelings and to "*apologize*" for seen and unforeseen incidents. Further, taking the blame for not learning the things we needed to have learned to make life easier; better and healthier for our self and loved ones is also reason to *apologize*.

For example, being a parent is not easy. Many challenges come with this title. Is there a wrong way, a better way, options or solutions to benefit from when rearing children? The answer is yes, and yes, to each of those. Think about it!

Whose fault was it that you were born in your family? You were dealt this specific life with no say so as to who or when. Whose fault was it that you picked up those genetic genes and heredities from the family line?

When I think of the above, I just want to say, I *apologize*. The hand you were dealt, well, you can't take it back. It is final! You have to live with it, you have to accept it, you have to manage it and you certainly have to bear it as best you can.

Oh, in case you were wondering, rich or poor, sick or in good health, good looking or not so good looking (beauty is in the eyes of the beholder); drugs or alcohol, male or female, straight or gay, it doesn't matter, life has a way of keeping us all on even ground. My example is this, heartache is heartache, worry is worry, frustrations are frustrations; never satisfied is just what it is never satisfied. What you have is never going to be enough, misery is real. Money cannot fix what I just described, good looks will not make it better, being sick or in good health won't change how it's never enough. Being and feeling unfulfilled is real, so real that you must encounter something supernatural to surpass these things. So I say again, life has a way of keeping us on even ground.

If your family is anything like mine, well, I have witnessed some stuff. I have experienced the highs and lows of "family." Single family parent, abuse, welfare, step dad, cut-off relationships, fighting, anger, mental disturbance, poor health, unhealthy relationships, poverty, etc., truth be told, this list can go on and on. So once again, I apologize!

You see, we each have our own cross to bear. We each have our own way of figuring this thing out. We each have to make a decision as best we can with the knowledge we have learned to better ourselves. I only know what I have been taught by observation; I only know what I have learned through personal experience; I only know what I have read from a book; I only know what my peers have shared with me and family has coerced me to say and do; I only know as much as I have sought to find out from the experts; I only know what I have been exposed to or the lack thereof. I only know... so for that, I apologize.

Are you up for growing pains? Are you ready to see what life is all about? Are you anticipating the unknown? Are you ready for the highs and lows of relationships? Are you fit for the course? Are you... are you... are you? Is there a prototype to follow; is there a mold made; has someone gone before you to figure out life? Will you be the first but certainly not the last? Do you have enough intelligence to find your way in this uncertain world?

Keep living and you will find out many of these answers. *ADULTING* **is real**! One way of learning or should I say consider reading the Book of Ecclesiastes. This book is full of insights and revelation knowledge. You will not be disappointed!

APOLOGIZE!

We all need to keep apologizing.
We all can use a helping hand.

We all have to face our music in this
dry and desert land.

Life has curves, bumps and hills to climb,
So get right down to it and escape
as best you can the grime.

Keep apologizing, apologizing, for
no one person has the key,

But if we apologize along the way
it can be contagious you see.

For if the truth be told, an apology
might be a good recipe,

A recipe for life, for humanity, and
even our souls;

A recipe for truth and every story
untold;

A recipe for love and an opportunity
to be different;

A recipe for each of us to recognize
our uniqueness,

So apologize, apologize and be free

To find out whom God intended
YOU to BE.

It is there you will find all of your
unanswered questions.

So, A.p.o.l.o.g.i.z.e...every
opportunity you get along the way

And BE your unique SELF.

Author: Robin A. Price-Boyd

WHY THE GUIDE?

From God's perspective, there is no other way. He always wants us to be blessed and safe. He always has our best interest at heart. He wants us to live an abundant life. He is simply a proactive God. Why do you think the Bible was written over 6,000 years ago and reaches out to every generation and Nation?

I often hear this saying amongst the Saints: the Bible letters mean: **"Basic Instructions Before Leaving Earth."** This I have found to be true! Below are a few things you should know about the Bible:

(1)   It is one of the oldest books that have ever been written.

(2)   It is passed down from one generation to the next.

- He talks about instructing us
- He talks about teaching us
- He talks about guiding us

Did you know that the Lord does the above three things for a specific reason? Let's find out why we need INSTRUCTION, why we need to be TAUGHT, and finally, why we need a GUIDE.

Instruction

Proverbs 10:17 says He/she is in the way of life that keeps instruction.

Proverbs 12:1 says Whoso loves instruction loves knowledge: but whoever hates reproof (correction) is brutish.

Proverbs 13:18 says Poverty and shame shall be to the person that refuses instruction: but whoever regards reproof (correction) shall be honored.

Proverbs 15:5 says A fool despises his father's instruction; but whosoever regards reproof is prudent.

Proverbs 15:10 says Correction is grievous unto a person who forsakes the way: and whosoever hates reproof shall die.

Proverbs 15:31 says "The ear that hears the reproof of life abides among the wise."

Proverbs 15:32 says the person that refuses instruction despises their own soul: but whosoever hears reproof gets understanding.

2 Timothy 3:16 says "All scripture is given by inspiration of God, and is profitable for doctrine, for reproof, for correction, for instruction in righteousness."

The word "**Instruction**" seems to be vital for our daily living. The word "**Reproof**" also has meaning in these passages of Scripture's as well. I don't know about you, but when I think of "instruction," I think of a classroom setting or learning about something unknown. For example how to put something together – furniture often times come with instructions, a manual or handbook for assembling. So likewise the Bible gives instructions for healthy living.

Teach

In the Old Testament, whenever God taught something to the children of Israel, His people, He would always tell them, "now teach it to your sons and daughters" (see Deuteronomy 4:9).

Psalm 25:4 says "Show me thy ways, O Lord; teach me thy paths."

Psalm 25:5 says Lead me in thy truth, and teach me…O' Lord.

Psalm 25:8 says "Good and upright is the Lord: therefore will he teach sinners in the way."

Psalm 27:11 says "Teach me thy way, O Lord, and lead me in a plain path, because of mine enemies" wow!

Psalm 34:11 says "Come, ye children, hearken unto me: I will teach you the fear of the Lord" (to Reverence God).

Psalm 119:26 says…teach me thy statutes (written law/regulation) in scripture.

Matthew 28:19 says Go ye therefore, and teach all nations (people)….

Simply put, we need to be taught the ways of God to obtain (1) the promises, and (2) the blessings that are written throughout His Word.

Guide

Psalm 48:14

For this *is* God...Our God forever and ever; He will be our **guide** e*ven* to death.

Psalm 73:24

God will guide "you" with His counsel~

Psalm 78:72

So he shepherded them according to the integrity of his heart, And **guide**d them by the skillfulness of his hands.

Psalm 107:30

...So He **guide**s us to our desired haven.

Psalm 112:5

A good person deals graciously and lends; He will **guide** his affairs with discretion.

Proverbs 11:3

The integrity of the upright **guides** them...

Proverbs 23:19

Are you open to **guide** your heart in the way of the Lord?

Isaiah 51:18

…the LORD will **guide** you continually, and satisfy your soul in drought, and strengthen your bones~

Jeremiah 3:4

He desires to **guide** you from youth~

Luke 1:79

He **guides** our feet into the way of peace~

John 16:13

He will **guide** you into all truth~.

So you see, we all need to be guided along this life's journey, no matter our age! God wants to be your personal tour guide through life; will you allow Him that opportunity?

BIBLE STUDY

Just in case you have never entered into a Church building, here is what a typical **Bible Study** would consist of:

A **corporate topic** of discussion for the audience (Body of Christ);

A **teaching of that topic** for growth and development~

A **Practical application example(s)** to help with walking out your life before God~

Then Fellowship with other believers so that you might witness and see how much we need one another~ Often times you discover that others are going through similar things that you are.

Last but not least, a sense of Encouragement and Joy to gain strength and confidence in a living God who so delicately speaks to us through the local Pastor or shepherd.

The first opportunity you get, I invite you to try attending a Bible Study in your area. Weigh the effects of coming together with other believers who love God. Rate your experience from 1 to 10 and then assess the benefits. Be honest and constructive!

Finally, talk with God about that experience and be open to returning to another bible study...who knows...there may be a personal word spoken to YOU!

Now let's look at a sample Bible Study message.

TOPIC: I SEE

One of the most profound things we can come to understand in the Bible as we learn of Jesus, and why He came into our "world," is that our eyes might be open to the TRUTH!

John 18:37

"To this end was I born, and for this cause came I into the world, that I should bear witness unto the **truth**." The writer further exclaims "Every one that is of the **truth** heareth my voice." God's voice through His Son Jesus is WRITTEN in the form of the Bible.

John 8:47

As a referenced scripture from John 18:37, Jesus further states, "He that is of God heareth God's words…"

As children of God, we do not question His WORD. Instead, we learn that the Bible is the **truth**. As we embrace the *truth*, signs, wonders, and miracles will manifest (be made known) in our lives. In other words, our spiritual eyes will be opened! God will confirm His word to you!

As a foundation to build upon from the **truth**, I felt it appropriate to start with these profound scriptures:

John 15:5b

...for without God, you and I can do nothing.

Acts 4:12

...for there is none other name under heaven given among men, whereby we must be saved.

Acts 17:28

For in Him (Jesus) we live, move, and have our being...

It's amazing how many people do not understand this *truth*.

Our journey of the **truth** is one of discovery. Often times this is why we walk through life having different experiences. Why we are exposed to different things. Why we are tailor-made even from our mother's womb. It's not by accident that your road-block is different from mine. **It's not by accident that your highs and lows in life are sometimes seemingly dark, but yet becomes colorful on the other end.**

Discovery is powerful! If you permit "discovery" to be a part of your life, you will find interesting answers to life's most complex questions. Your uniqueness and peculiar way is not surprising to God. Therefore, learn to be true to you! Do not worry about the next person and what he or she might think of you. We are all different, unique and peculiar. Each of us brings something special to contribute in the world.

The happiest person is one who can embrace their uniqueness, their peculiar ways, their awkwardness. After all, the scripture tells us that we each are fearfully and wonderful made (Psalm 139:14); that we were made in secret (Psalm 139:15); that our inward parts while in secret were fashioned (Psalm 139:16). Everything about you can be defined through scriptures…so discover that He (Jesus) came to make known the *TRUTH*.

What you should know about the *TRUTH:*

2 Corinthians 13:8 states, "For we can do nothing against the **truth**, but for the truth."

Proverbs 23:23 states, "Buy the **truth**, and sell it not; also wisdom, and instruction, and understanding."

John 8:31-32 states, (I am paraphrasing this one), "if you stay in God's word, to read it, meditate in it and study it, you will become a learner and student of God indeed; and you will discover the **truth**, and the **truth** will set you free." How awesome!

I cannot imagine being in the earth for any amount of time or space and never embracing the "truth." It's amazing what "time" reveals to each of us. The truth is not difficult to find when you seek it with all your heart, mind, and soul. We were never created to be in the dark for long periods of time; but that light might shine on our darkness to bring revelation and insight to the truth. Remember, one of the reasons Jesus came was to bear witness to the truth.

During your journey of discovery, things will happen to enlighten your eyes, to change your heart, and to transform your mind. What you believed three (3) years ago will dramatically change in some way. Life and its experiences will teach you something different. Don't take my word for it; live and you will see. Ask someone you know and trust, what they have learned different from three years ago? What happened or changed? Listen carefully and you will learn something.

The title of this Bible Study "**I See**," was simply to engage the audience (you) to think about life, where you are, where you are headed, what lies ahead in your tomorrow, and future. It's not by happenstance that you are even reading this book. Often times, we open new doors of learning because of our increased level of **Consciousness**, **Curiosity**, and a desire for **Change** (The 3 C's).

The Bible can be refreshing and provoking at the same time. It is an eye opener, and yes, the Word of God tugs at our heart.

Scripture puts it this way in Hebrews 4:12, "it (the Bible) is a discerner of our thoughts and intents of our heart." The book is simply quite candid about life. So, get a glass of lemonade, milk or coffee, relax and go to it... with reading that is, and let God reveal answers to your questions, solutions to your problems, and give wisdom to your everyday concerns. I personally cannot wait for you to discover the things that He gives...wow, are you in for a delightful surprise.

Note, Bible Studies throughout this book are designed to provoke you to discover the TRUTH about everything and anything your little heart can desire to know.

Because Jesus came, you (we) have an opportunity to know all things!

This lesson was designed to be short, insightful, inspirational and impactful for YOU, the reader.

My Prayer for YOU:
Lord, as this reader engages and yearns to know more about you; your Word and the Truth; open his or her eyes. *In Jesus Name*, Amen!

DISCOVERY

While reading the Word today, I thought about how the Lord took time to drop nuggets in the Bible regarding his human side. How He decided to reveal a little bit about who HE was and how He could relate to us, His creation. It only took one word **clothed**, and my eyes were opened.

Psalm 104:1 states the following, "Bless the Lord, O my soul, O Lord my God, thou art very great; thou art _clothed_ with honor and majesty." Verse 2 states, "Who coverest thyself with light and a garment, who stretches out the heavens like a curtain." Hum! Did you catch that? God's "**choice**" words tell us something, doesn't it? 1 Peter 5:5 says we are _clothed_ with humility. Humility is a state of lowliness in heart...not arrogant or being proud.

You see how God was having a conversation with us through the writer of Psalm to give us a glimpse of Himself... _clothed_ with honor and majesty. How awesome, do you recall in an earlier chapter (page 22) we discussed how we were made in his likeness and in his image? Now today, presently, I am still finding clues in the Word of God (the Bible) for us to discover who He is. I call something like this, finding a needle in the haystack! ☺

Deuteronomy 29:29 states, "the secret things belong unto the Lord our God: but those things which are _revealed_ belong unto us and to our children for ever; that we may do all the words of this law" (the Bible). The needle in the haystack, well, that is something like a secret being discovered is it not?

Ladies and gentlemen, that is why we read the Word. It is there we discover and uncover things. It is in the Word that our eyes are opened. It is there that we read of God's most revealing secrets...the Bible even calls them mysteries. I found at least 20 mysteries in the Word of God. So be open, explore life, and find out the mysteries of the Kingdom of Heaven and of God. Pick up the Bible and begin your journey of discovery of who God is. Begin your personal relationship today with Him.

Scripture tells us in *Romans 10:9-10*, that "if we confess with our mouth the Lord Jesus, and shall believe in our heart that God has raised Jesus from the dead, we shall be saved." Do you believe this? Romans 10:10 states, "for with the heart man/woman believes unto righteousness; and with the mouth confession is made unto salvation." It's that simple!

Think about it for a moment, when you believe something whole heartedly, you talk about it, you share it with others; you confess it with your own lips, right? Well the same thing occurs with God's Word; nothing's different. Your own personal experiences in life and your encounters with a living God will help you to come to this realization and truth.

I will never forget the time God saved me from a car accident, it was unexplainable, it was supernatural; it was unbelievable! That is the kind of testimony that our Heavenly Father will leave with us... pretty much speechless and in **Awe of Him**! When divinity touches from heaven to earth, you no doubt will have something to testify about, you will know that you have come into the realm of the supernatural! Glory Be to God!

FORGIVE ME!

Why is it difficult for you to believe that others care about you, about your welfare, about your tomorrow, about the path you are currently traveling. The fact that you are God's creation and His handy work, you matter! Love has no favorites and creates space for everyone! The TRUTH is in the earth for a reason. You were not an accident; you have a purpose!

Forgive me if I care. *Forgive* me if I invade your space for a moment to voice a thought that I believe is worth voicing. After all, I function better when I see injustice. I dislike when others are being picked on. I am annoyed with those who believe they are better than others. I get irritated when I see someone taking advantage of a less fortunate person. It's insulting to see "some" discriminated against.

So yes, **forgive** me if you matter. When God sees injustice - whether by an individual of high degree (position or prominence), a boss or supervisor or by someone of excessive force (police), misconduct, profiling, harassment, homicides - you can be sure to know, they have not gotten away with it. There is an appointed time for justice to be served. God's timing is not our timing. His ways are far above our ways (see Isaiah 55:9).

The fact that God has angels on earth tending to His business (you); the fact that you have a purpose in life and not yet in pursuit of that purpose…doesn't mean that the Lord will not attempt to reach you. Love doesn't give up! As a matter of fact, you will learn that Love is patient, Love is kind,

Love endures; Love does not think ill or gives up on you (1 Corinthians Chapter 13).

As I respect your approach to life, and believe you will find your way, allow others to care for you. Granted, sometimes love ones show their caring in different ways...however, true Love – _agape_ love bears all things, believes all things and hopes for all things (1 Corinthians Ch. 13). This kind of unconditional Love might be beyond your present comprehension or understanding. But rest assured one day you will come into the knowledge of this truth. Believe me no one wants to run your life, truth be told, we have our own concerns to contend with on a daily basis.

Well it's been months since I last picked up this book, "The Guide." So much has happened over this span of time. You see, for the past few years, I have worked in the public school system to experience what school life is about and what you as students have had to endure, and likewise the teachers and educators. From the Alternative (Community) school, to Middle school, to Elementary school and finally to High school, ultimately back to the Community school. I have literally been full circle.

By far, my experience in the Middle school has been the most interesting. Surprisingly, these students were more...

- Disrespectful
- Angry
- Defiant
- Resistant
- Attitudes (poor)
- Talkative /talk back
- Vulgar/used of profanity
- Unsettled & restless
- And more...

I have never seen anything like it! School for many students has become a social gathering place; academics are the last thing seemingly on their mind. Some young people simply dislike school! Some students have not a clue that education is a ticket to a better way of living. There is truly a disconnection to fully understanding the advantage of what a good education can do for you.

I have witnessed with my own eyes, how there is a distasteful appetite for learning in a regular classroom setting. Some students would have truly benefited better from a (1) Montessori learning environment while others would have done better in a (2) home school setting; and yet, I witnessed others needing assistance from a (3) smaller class room setting to focus and learn! Understanding how students learn is important for teachers to discern.

What are you as a young person crying for? What can be done to alter your path for greater impact of development: academically, spiritually, mentally, emotionally, relationally and physically. One has to wonder what are you crying for, what needs are missing, how might educators begin to see through your eyes or window pane and make that adjustment to help you. Mind you, there is limited space in which we (teachers) participate. Counselors, family, friends, the community (agencies) and others will have to do their part as well. A school learning environment typically helps to develop ones "Academics" but impacts other components of life as well.

This is not to say that Elementary or High school students do not have issues. What I am saying is this, that Middle school students have been the worse of the three school settings I have worked. Why is that?

Back in the day, I could not have imagined acting out as our young people do today in school. Thus, every opportunity I have today to impact a child, I try to take advantage of that moment. For example: with any level of resistance (defiance, disrespect, profanity, talk back, etc.), I present each student with a _consequence_. In my own way, I let it be known that poor behavior was and is not acceptable in a learning environment. Why, because I care about their (your) future!

We (teachers) do you (students) an injustice by tolerating "behavior" or by excusing "behavior" that is not conducive to a learning environment. Teachers should not be passive but proactive all the time. Life is full of choices, and with those choices, comes a resounding _Consequence_. If young people (YOU) learn this lesson early on in life, just maybe better choices will be made. Therefore, FORGIVE me (us) teachers, parents, counselors, etc., for not making this truth known about _consequences_. FORGIVE us for not holding you accountable when you act out.

The Bible gives us information about "Sowing" and "Reaping." Sowing and reaping is likened to "Choices" and "Consequences." You "Choose" but you have no say so in the "Consequence." If you sow good, good will come back to you; if you sow bad however, bad will come back to you. Good choices bring a good outcome; likewise bad choices will reap bad outcomes. Why is this important? I thought you would never ask… In and of itself, you control your future, you control your destiny; you have direct impact on what the results will be for a measure of what is being dealt to you on a daily basis. There are some levels or measures of control that are designed by your hand, work, ways and choices.

The following passages of Scripture will help give insight to a truth that you will discover along your life journey. Consider keeping a record or journal of decisions you make for the next 30 days. Jot down the date, the decision you made (good or poor) and wait for the outcome to manifest, keeping in mind the following scriptures:

(1)   **Romans 2:6** states that to whatever you render out to a person, the Lord will deal with you according to your _deed_ done~

(2)   **Proverbs 24:12** states that to whatever you render out to a person, the Lord will deal with you according to your _work_ done.

(3)   **Psalm 28:4** states that to whatever you render out to a person, the Lord will deal with you according to your *endeavors*, deeds and work done.

(4)   **Isaiah 3:10** states that a good person shall reap the fruit of their *doings.*

Everything we do – our deeds, our works, our endeavors, our ways and our doings – shall be dealt or measured back unto us. He concludes the matter by giving us this insight in *Galatians 6:7* stating, "be not deceived; God is not mocked: for whatsoever a person sow, that shall he or she also reap."   That you can trust, so reflect, meditate, and ponder on your decisions going forward. What you have encountered at home, at school, amongst your peers, in the community, ponder and see if what I am saying is the truth. Keep your heart/mind clean and free by doing well!   Learn to do unto to others as you would have them to do unto you. This is a safe practice moving forward! The ball is in your court...control your destiny by making better/wise decisions starting today.

I have a question for you? What did you or others think you were getting away with by acting out? Be it in grade school, middle school or high school. Think about the behaviors mentioned earlier. Was that you? Did you know of someone who acted out in that way?

Are you presently a middle, high school, or college student now with similar behaviors? What do you recommend as consequences for yourself and others who demonstrate these poor behaviors? How has your attitude played a part in your behavior?

List here in the space below:

1. _____
2. _____
3. _____
4. _____

How has dad or mom, the principal, teachers and others attempted to manage your poor behavior of acting out? Were there consequences or did you get away with the behavior? Allow me to share this little secret, God saw your behavior (acting out), the deed, endeavor, work or your doings.

So you see; school life can make a great testing ground for you to discover things, real things, practical things, and even principles of life. From this time forward, learn well, grow well and prepare well for what's to come in days ahead in your life.

Now for practical application, consider completing an exercise with a close friend. Team up with someone you know who will hold you accountable for your poor behavior. Take note of your behavior for 30 days in school and at home. Document the situation, the behavior, the consequence if any and track your outcome (what was gained or loss?)

Write the situation here:

_____

_____

_____

_____

_____

_____

How did you respond (Behavior)?

1. Disrespectful _____
2. Angry
3. Defiant _____
4. Resistant _____
5. Attitude _____
6. Talk Back / Last Word _____
7. Vulgar/use of profanity _____
8. Tantrum _____
9. Other _____ _____

What was the Consequence?

No Consequence　　　＿＿＿＿
Yes Consequence　　　＿＿＿＿

Write your outcome here (you gained or you loss what), did you care?

_____

_____

_____

_____

_____

_____

_____

_____

_____

_____

_____

_____.

If you did not care...well, you might have been plagued with a poor attitude.

PEER PRESSURE

Truly there is nothing new under the sun! When I stumbled onto this passage of Scripture while reading, I thought it was funny. The Bible was written back in 1600 A.D. and yet it is relevant to today. One of the disciples' of Jesus Christ had a real experience with *Peer Pressure*.

Listen to this encounter found in Galatians Chapter 2, verse 11 – 13: "Later, when Peter came to Antioch, I (Paul) had a face-to-face **confrontation** with him because he was clearly out of line." Here's the situation. Earlier, before certain persons had come to James, Peter regularly ate with the non-Jews. But when a conservative group came from Jerusalem, he cautiously **pulled back** and put as much distance as he could between himself and his non-Jewish friends. That's how **fearful** Peter was of the conservative Jewish **clique** who had been pushing the old law of circumcision. (_Natural circumcision: for Males is the surgical removal of the foreskin from the genital private part. Spiritual circumcision dealt with a believer having a changed heart, resulting in a new state of mind_). Unfortunately, the rest of the Jews in the Antioch church joined in that **hypocrisy** so that even Barnabas (another disciple of Christ) was swept along in the masquerade.

[14] "But when I saw that they were not maintaining a steady, straight course according to the Message (doctrine), I spoke up to Peter in front of them all: "If you, a Jew, live like a non-Jew when you're not being observed by the watchdogs from Jerusalem, what right do you have to require non-Jews to conform to Jewish customs just

to make a favorable impression on your old Jerusalem cronies?"☺ Wow! A leader with guts asking a bold question!

I found this encounter interesting, how James called Peter out. How James made Peter accountable for his actions in front of his peers... the clique... the up to do ones. We see that today, don't we? So again I say; *there is nothing new under the sun.* **Peer pressure is real**. We no doubt will experience *peer pressure* time and time again, but how will we (you) handle it?

You can make a "statement" when faced with *Peer Pressure*. You can determine in your heart not to back down but to hold your peers accountable to do the right thing. When faced with an encounter of your own, be brave, be courageous; be encouraged to do what's right... *let your conscience (heart) guide you;* Do unto others as you would have them to do unto you! One other thing, did you note the terms used in this Bible story? Terms like Confrontation, Clique, Fear, and Hypocrisy. Be prepared and familiarize yourself with these terms for future reference. Look up these words and hide them in your heart. Be ready to resist any temptation…do not bow or give in to *peer pressure moments* when they come. Note I stated when it comes, not if it comes. As new believer, God will back you! He will support your right decision.

Who is Really in Control?

The good Book of Wisdom reveals something very interesting in Ephesians 2:2. When I read this verse, my eyes were opened. Here is how it reads; "wherein time past you walked according to the course of this world, according to the prince of the power of the air, the spirit that now works in disobedient children."

What do you mean we walk according to the course of this world; according to a higher power that rules the atmosphere...a force that influences our decision making and choices? Thank you! I am glad you asked that question☺. Believe it or not, your fleshly appetite for pleasing self, your fleshy desires (over indulging), and your selfish whims are influenced daily by a higher power. Here is how this works: when you would do right, wrong seems to be the outcome. For the good you intended to perform, well... you seem to fall short of doing it. The inward battle is real! The fight between the flesh and spirit is inevitable! Fulfilling the lust of the flesh, fulfilling the lust of the eyes, and walking in the pride of life unleashes our battles. Why, because the lust of the flesh, the lust of eyes and the pride of life is contrary to the **will of God.**

Have you ever wondered why it is difficult to stop smoking, to turn from drugs or alcohol, to resist sexual sins, to control your appetites or over indulging of any sort? What you feed grows. The doors you open are of **choice**. Pleasures of the flesh are costly! Without any resistance, without the power of God to help, without surrendering your will of choice, you will encounter great challenges. *So again I ask; who is really in control?*

Romans 7:15-20
(The Message Bible (MSG)

"I can anticipate the response that is coming: "I know that all God's commands are spiritual, but I'm not. Isn't this also your experience?" Yes. I'm full of myself—after all, I've spent a long time in sin's prison. What I don't understand about myself is that I decide one way, but then I act another, doing things I absolutely despise. So if I can't be trusted to figure out what is best for my-self and then do it, it becomes obvious that God's command is necessary."

"But I need something *more*! For if I know the law but still can't keep it, and if the power of sin within me keeps sabotaging my best intentions, I obviously need help! I realize that I don't have what it takes. I can will it, but I can't *do* it. I decide to do good...but I don't *really* do it; I decide not to do wrong but then I do it anyway. My decisions, such as they are, don't result in actions. Something has gone wrong deep within me and gets the better of me every time." Wow! *So again I ask you; who is really in control?*

Another scripture to put in the mix of this conversation is found in **Proverbs 21:1**. God is in control and has the final say in many of our outcomes. Why? Because the king's heart is in the hand of the Lord, as the rivers of water flow downstream: God turns the King's heart whithersoever he will. Hmm! *Once again, I ask you; who is really in control?*

With that said, does the Judge have the final say so in the court room? Does the teacher give the final grade at school? Does the police officer really write the ticket? Is mom or dad giving the instructions around the house? A just God is He. The Lord rewards righteous living (uprightness). He is fair and takes pleasure in rewarding those who reverence Him. Please refer back to (Sowing and reaping).

The Message Bible (MSG) states in **Proverbs 16:9**, "we plan the way we want to live, but only GOD makes us able to live it.

How about this scripture in **Job 3:23**, "Why is light given to a person whose way is hid, and whom God hath hedged in?" I don't care where you are in life; one has to wonder are you really in control? As you travel on your life journey, your path is designed for you to discover this truth (you are not in control). Ecclesiastes chapter 3 talks of 28 seasons you and I will encounter throughout life. These seasons are not by happenstance, but are strategic by God for us to learn about Him, to seek His face; to understand He controls all things.

As an exercise, keep account and/or examine your life going forward to see if what I am saying is real or no. Learn to make right choices for better outcomes, right choices for better consequences, right choices to experience a better quality of life. Jot down your discovery along the way. Are you in control of your life or not? See how you fair as you complete this exercise. If you have any questions, please feel free to email me (see email address at end of book).

WALK SOFTLY, SPEAK SOFTLY AND CHOOSE WISELY ALONG THIS JOURNEY~

Never in a million years would I have thought that my student (17 years of age) was in his last days. It was a blind spot. The news was shocking, unbelievable, insane, unfathomed; I was in disbelief when I received the call. But why, the book of Wisdom already warns us that no man or woman knows the day, the hour, the minute or second when he or she will leave this earth. And yet, it was an element of surprise for me.

Some would say: he lived a lifestyle that predicted his outcome, he was his own man; he walked a life contrary to longevity. And yet, it shook everyone; the Principal, the teachers, his peers and classmates and of course his family and friends. Hindsight, you learn more of a person when he or she is removed from this earth. The whispers, the rumors, the kind and unkind thoughts of others seemingly just poured out. I wonder could anyone have helped, did anyone even care enough to help; was his case over before a trial could began? Right now, all I know was that a life was snuffed out right before our eyes. A soul with intellect and intelligence, a soul with emotions and feelings, a soul with a will to do right or to do wrong, left this earth prematurely.

I heard one young man ask this question, who will be next? That was the talk in the hallways at high schools; in the bathrooms, out on the yard; who is going to be next? Some even placed a name in the position of N E X T. How dare them to make such a prediction on "life," someone else's "life." All I know is that this young man died a senseless death. There was no value placed on his life, his purpose was sifted out right from underneath him. The "shooter," "killer," "adversary," had no vision for who this young man could have become.

My glimpse, he was intelligent, bright, and an A – B student. He was a young man with possibilities, a young man with a family who loved him (imperfection and all), a young heart that was vibrant with energy, and a temperament that needed harnessing. What could have become of that? Do you dare to make an educated guess?

Many were sadden by the tragedy, mourned, hurt, angry, grieved, and lost for words over the death of this young man. This kid who tried to live in a grown man's position never understood his consequences for the life he was living. The consequences were costly for his actions! Unfortunately, this kid grew up without a father. He learned from the streets and connected with the wrong people! His lifestyle was that of riotous living! He failed to take heed to his warning signs and not to hear wisdom. He was influenced by the wrong crowd!

This young man will never have a legacy to live on after him. He will never have children to carry on his name. He can never fulfill his true purpose which was given him in Christ Jesus before the foundation of the world (2 Timothy 1:9). He now joins a host of young men whose blood cries from the ground. I am reminded of a story in the Bible that often repeats itself in the earth today. Have you heard about it? The story about Cane and Abel that is in **Genesis 4:8-10**. Well, if you haven't, let me share this story with you now.

This story comes out of the book of Genesis (the beginning), how relevant, how profound, how timeless a word from God to speak in right now situations long ago. Genesis 4:8-10 tells of a story between two souls (kin folks...brothers). The dividing line between these two brothers were: (1) jealousy, (2) anger, (3) hatred; we call it as the Bible calls it, SIN.

Cain rose up against his brother Abel and slew him while in the field. If you read this story from the beginning, you learn that God had a conversation with Cain prior to him killing his brother (Abel). In Genesis 4:6, God asked Cain why was he angry, why was he throwing a tantrum, why was his countenance fallen (as in defeat)? In verse 7, God continues to converse with Cain and states the following: "if you do well (live right); you shall be accepted (validated), but if you do wrong, trouble awaits you," you will pay for your wrong. And then, God challenges Cain to overcome his evil thoughts... sin... shortfall. You see, killing his brother Abel was a choice!

Instead of taking heed to the counsel of God, Cain responds by doing the unthinkable. He coerces his brother (being deceitful) to go out into a field to harm him in Genesis 4:8. The verse reads as follows: "Cain talked with Abel his brother: and it came to pass, when they were in the field, that Cain rose up against Abel his brother, and slew him." That's crazy! Obviously, something was going on in Cain's heart that God could see... motives and intent perhaps, ill will and discontentment maybe, sin. Cain was missing the mark from walking upright before God. You know the saying, actions speaks louder than words!

God continues to ask Cain questions in verse 9, "And the Lord said unto Cain, Where is Abel thy brother? And he said; I know not: Am I my brother's keeper? Wow! Was Cain being smart with God? Did Cain lie?

Here is where I am going with this story, verse 10 depicts when innocent blood is shed by the hand of another person what happens in the "spirit" realm. "And God said what have you done? The voice of your brother's blood cries unto me from the ground." **And immediately, Cain was judged and cursed.** *Nothing gets by God!* Cain pre-meditated the murder of his brother. Young people, consequences are real!

The condition of Cain's heart was bad, rotten and sinful. You and I know when we are not in the right spirit, when we are thinking wrong, when our thoughts run away from us...do we not? Starting today, begin to manage your thought life better. Starting today, try controlling your feelings and emotions before acting on them. In case you did not know this, your thought life stimulates your feelings/emotions and thus causes you to behave or act out (positively or negatively). You and I are wired to think, feel and then behave! In that order!

Thus, walk softly...speak softly and choose wisely along the way. Take heed to warnings, listen to your conscience... avoid people who have demonstrated evil and proven to live unfruitful lives. Connect to life and not death. What do I mean by that? I thought you would never ask...connect to life, people and things that are edifying, people and things that are encouraging, people and things that will lift your spirits and build you up.

Contrary, stay away from negativity, from things that pull you down, from people that mean you no good and that bring drama in your life. Do not speak anything negative! The good book of Wisdom puts it this way in **Proverbs 18:21**, words kill, words give life; they're either poison or fruit – you choose" (*MSG Bible*). "Death and life are in the power of the tongue: and they that love it shall eat the fruit thereof" (*KJV*).

Now is a good time to inventory your list of friends and associates to see if you are surrounded by positive, productive, and kind people. Make a choice. Abort or run from those who mean you no good, who will damage your reputation; who will place you in harm way. The student who lost his life at seventeen years of age walked contrary to God's will. His choices cost him his life. His untimely death saddened the community and devastated his family. At present, those who committed the murder have been sentenced by a court of law and are now serving time in the penitentiary. The Lord will avenge us! Learn to **stop** taking matters into your own hands!

Romans 12:19

Dearly beloved, avenge not yourselves, but rather give place unto wrath: for it is written, VENGEANCE IS MINE; I WILL REPAY, saith the Lord (KJV).

~Its God's way, Its God's timing not ours~

And the Truth shall make you Free!

Final Thoughts!

You are not alone! Because it is important for you to walk out your life and to discover your fate, trial and error will be a part of your process. Since you will be learning and attempting to figure things out, why not begin something new along the way. I would like to introduce you to "**Well Doing**."

Well doing is something that every person can participate in on a daily basis. The power of "**well doing**" is that with each situation you face, with every dilemma met, for every obstacle encountered, you can choose to **do well**. You can choose to **do well** with the person involved, with the event at hand, with the decision that has to be made, and for the desired outcome. **Doing well** is catchy! **Doing well** brings favorable results! **Doing well** draws an

The Guide

audience! **Doing well** speaks volume to others without you having to open your mouth!

The Bible speaks to "**doing well!**" **Galatians 6:9** says, "And let us not be weary in *well doing*: for in due season we shall reap, if we faint not." **Doing well** is something you can plan for and intentionally set out to do on a daily basis...never letting up! We are called to *do well* with patient continuance according to **Romans 2:6-11**.

We are called to *do well* to put others to silence for their ignorance of the truth, see **1 Peter 2:15-16**.

We are called to *do well* with some suffering as we trust in the living God. In **1 Peter 3:17** it says, it is the will of God that we suffer for *well doing*, rather than for evil doing...ponder that for moment. God's grace helps us in those trying moments☺.

In keeping in line with this theme, let's remember that we are accountable for our actions be it good or bad. Remember, God rewards each of us according to:

(1)   Our ways

(2)   Our deeds

(3)   Our endeavors

(4)   Our work

(5)   The fruit of our doing &

(6)   Our righteousness

With that said, it behooves each of us to *do well every day,* and to maintain the right perspective for why we do what we do. You are blessed and can live a prosperous life in Jesus! Choose to live a life pleasing unto Him. Read *Romans 10:9-10*; then tell a friend and find a Church home! Your confession is important to your declaration and decision. God the Father will meet you on the other side of your decision. Prayers are already in motion for YOU! Keep the

GUIDE BOOK close but also be ready to start your journey in God's WORD! In the New Testament, the book of Matthew, Mark, Luke and John awaits YOU! ☺ Begin your personal relationship with Jesus by getting to know who He is and why He came to earth to save YOU, us. I promise He is REAL!

PRAYER

Lord, bless every reader and draw them into your fold by your Spirit.

Lord, keep the minds and hearts of every person who reads "the Guide."

Lord, make yourself real unto them as you did for me, in Jesus Name I pray, Amen!

~Thank you Father~

Contact Information

Please feel free to write or email using the information below:

Website: www.robinprice-boyd.com

Email: inspiredcreations.price@gmail.com

Write: The Guide Book
P.O. Box 1039
Elizabeth City, NC 27909

Attention: Robin Price-Boyd

Made in the USA
Middletown, DE
23 March 2019